Apostasy in the Pulpit

and

Apathy in the Pews

*A Study in
the Book of Jude*

by

Guy Lee, D.D.

Apostasy in the Pulpit
and
Apathy in the Pews

*A Study in
the Book of Jude*

by
Guy Lee, D.D.
37 Bill Presley Road
Cleveland, GA 30528

Phone: 706-865-4555

E-mail: **tometterlee@gmail.com**

ISBN 978-1-7347481-0-9

Published
by
The Old Paths Publications, Inc.
142 Gold Flume Way
Cleveland, GA 30528
www.theoldpathspublications.com
TOP@theoldpathspublications.com

FOREWORD

The book of Jude is small, but it is packed full of warnings and insight about the apostasy of the last days.

Guy has written his little book, *Apostasy in the Pulpit and Apathy in the Pews*, to explain and share the urgency that Jude did so long ago. He warns us to be aware, to be informed, and to be involved. To be forewarned is to be forearmed. We cannot be neutral in these last days.

Thank you Guy for your time, study, help, and example of what to do in this world in which we live. You are truly an authentic example of how we are to fight for the faith.

Dr. Tom Etterlee
March 2020

TABLE OF CONTENTS

INTRODUCTION

I am grateful to the Lord for His help in the completion of this book on the book of Jude. It is my earnest hope that it will be a help to the Lord's people in a further appreciation for the Word of God.

I am aware that the subjects of fallen angels mentioned in Jude verses 6 and 7, and II Peter 2:4 are quite controversial and that my treatment of them may not endear me to many beloved brethren.

Through much prayer and study, I have tried hard to speak the truth in love in this book and can only hope that the reader may be able to receive it.

Many years ago, Augustine of Hippo, better known as Saint Augustine, made a statement about what attitude we should take when we differ in the body of Christ. Quote from Augustine of Hippo:

"In essentials, unity; in non-essentials, liberty; in all things, charity."

Dr. Guy Lee
March 2020

Chapter 1

The epistle of Jude deals primarily with apostasy. It presents Old Testament examples of those who corrupted the faith, and it predicts God's judgment at the appearing of our Lord's return to the earth. Apostasy is here shown to be a willful return to ungodliness.

I. *Descendants – vs. 1*

Jude's mother, brothers, and sisters are recorded in Matthew 13:55-56, and Mark 6:3 that the writer Jude is a half-brother of Jesus.

- **Matthew 13:55** Is not this the carpenter's son? is not his mother called Mary? and his brethren, James, and Joses, and Simon, and Judas?
- **Matthew 13:56** And his sisters, are they not all with us? Whence then hath this *man* all these things?

- **Mark 6:3** Is not this the carpenter, the son of Mary, the brother of James, and Joses, and of Juda, and Simon?

This is the best explanation of the two phrases in his introduction.

First, he calls himself a servant of Jesus Christ. Jude simply calls himself a "servant" meaning a bond slave.

The second phrase identifies Jude as the brother of James. There is only one person in the New Testament Church whom everyone would know as just "James" and that was the brother of Jesus.

- **Galatians 1:19** But other of the apostles saw I none, save James the Lord's brother.

But another question may occur to us. If Jude is the half-brother of Jesus, why doesn't he say so straight out? The answer is probably twofold.

First, Jude recognizes that the physical ties of blood and genetics are of no eternal value. The spiritual tie with Jesus is what saves us.

Second, humility is also involved. Humility forbids Jude from mentioning himself as a physical half-brother of Jesus.

Joseph was Jude's father, but it was by the power of the Holy Spirit that Jesus was conceived in Mary's womb. Jesus is the eternal Son of God. Knowing that Jesus is Lord and God, Jude does not want to give any impression of being equal with Jesus. Announcing himself as being from the same family as Jesus could be misunderstood in such a way and Jude wishes to avoid that. So, he just calls himself a servant of Jesus Christ and a brother of James. Jude's name means praise.

A. Description – *vs. 1*

Jude gives us three remarkable descriptions of what it means to be a Christian.

1. Sanctification

"To them that are sanctified by God the Father"
The word sanctify means to set apart for God. Christians are vessels of honor for the Master's use.

- **II Timothy 2:2** If a man therefore purge himself from these, he shall be a vessel unto honour, sanctified, and meet for the master's use, *and* prepared unto every good work.

We are to do all for God's glory whether it is eating, drinking, or working.

- **I Corinthians 10:31** Whether therefore ye eat, or drink, or whatsoever ye do, do all to the glory of God.

2. Preserved in Jesus Christ

What an assuring word in the midst of a great apostasy as one considers the apostasy of angels and men! The word preserved means kept, provides comfort and assurance. Believers are kept by the power of God.

- **I Peter 1:5** Who are kept by the power of God through faith unto salvation ready to be revealed in the last time.

In the midst of all the difficulties and dangers that we face today, the Christian has a place of security in Christ. We are preserved by the same One that has saved us. We are kept by Christ and in Christ.

Wherefore, he is able also to save them to the uttermost that come unto God by Him (Jesus) seeing he ever liveth to make intercession for them.

- **Hebrews 7:25** Wherefore he is able also to save them to the uttermost that come unto God by him, seeing he ever liveth to make intercession for them.

The Greek word "uttermost" means all and complete. It involves the arrival at the final destination with all aspects of the believer completed spiritually.

3. Called

God's people are said to be called of Jesus Christ.

- **Romans 1:6** Among whom are ye also the called of Jesus Christ:

They are saints by calling.

- **I Corinthians 1:2** Unto the church of God which is at Corinth, to them that are sanctified in Christ Jesus, called *to be* saints, with all that in every place call upon the name of Jesus Christ our Lord, both theirs and ours:

God's children are a called people because all they have and enjoy is from The Lord himself. They are called from self to Christ and from sin to holiness.

a. God by His Spirit has called us out of darkness into His marvelous light.

- **I Peter 2:9** God *is* faithful, by whom ye were called unto the fellowship of his Son Jesus Christ our Lord.

b. It is a heavenly calling

- **Hebrews 3:1** Wherefore, holy brethren, partakers of the heavenly calling, consider the Apostle and High Priest of our profession, Christ Jesus;

c. It is a holy calling

- **II Timothy 1:9** Who hath saved us, and called *us* with an holy calling, not according to our works, but according to his own purpose and grace, which was given us in Christ Jesus before the world began,

d. It is a high calling

- **Philippians 3:14** I press toward the mark for the prize of the high calling of God in Christ Jesus.

Chapter 2

II. Desire – vs. 2

Jude desires a threefold blessing for his readers.

1. Mercy

Mercy is a perfection of God and is revealed in a special manner through Jesus Christ to all believers. We need redeeming mercy, eternal mercy, daily mercies, and future mercy.

2. Peace

There is a two-fold peace.

    a. Peace with God through Jesus Christ

- **Romans 5:1** Therefore being justified by faith, we have peace with God through our Lord Jesus Christ:

This points to the condition of well-being and inner peace that comes to those that have been reconciled to God.

    a. Peace of God

- **Philippians 4:7** And the peace of God, which passeth all understanding, shall keep your hearts and minds through Christ Jesus.

Future, in outworking in our Christian lives, we experience that peace through faith in Jesus Christ. There may be troubles in our personal lives, or the Church itself may be attacked physically and violently, but Jesus said "the gates of hell shall not prevail against it".

- **Matthew 16:18** And I say also unto thee, That thou art Peter, and upon this rock I will build my church; and the gates of hell shall not prevail against it.

Therefore, there is the peace of God which passes all understanding, which we can know as we commit our lives to Him and trust His promises.

- **Philippians 4:7** And the peace of God, which passeth all understanding, shall keep your hearts and minds through Christ Jesus.

3. Love

Love is understood as that of God toward men as well as that of men toward God and toward one another. It is impossible to have one without the other.

- **I John 1:7** But if we walk in the light, as he is in the light, we have fellowship one with another, and the blood of Jesus Christ his Son cleanseth us from all sin.
- **I John 1:8** If we say that we have no sin, we deceive ourselves, and the truth is not in us.

The word Jude uses for love is the Greek word agape. It is a term which applies to God. It is a love which is unconditional and even embraces the unlovely and the undeserving.

Chapter 3

III. Diligence – vs. 3

1. Common Salvation

"Beloved" is a glorious title. The Greek word "agape" speaks of Divine love, never changing. It is the love of John 3:16. God demonstrated that love at Calvary when He sent His Son to die as our substitute.

- **Romans 5:8** But God commendeth his love toward us, in that, while we were yet sinners, Christ died for us.

Diligence means "to desire earnestly". Jude was diligently preparing to write about our common salvation. The salvation we have in Christ is not in the sense that it is cheap, or of little use. It is an expression which means "to become a sharer, a partner". The idea is of "a common salvation" possessed in common with others. All who have been saved, have been saved by grace through faith in Christ. Thus, it is common to every believer.

2. Contend for the Faith

Jude had originally intended to write a letter containing a positive presentation of the doctrines of the Christian faith. The Holy Spirit lain upon his heart the necessity of writing in defense of the Faith.

Contend means to struggle for, fervently, strive. It speaks of a vigorous, intense, determined struggle to defeat the opposition.

We must contend for the original faith of the Gospel which is being attacked today by false teachers that we might not endanger the truth. Uncontrolled error will affect both the present and the next generation. We must take a stand for the truth no matter what the cost.

3. Consummation

Once, means once and for all. Jude declared that this was once, final, and without change. Every effort has been made throughout the centuries to destroy God's Word by banning, burning, or bending it. Today men seek to destroy The Scriptures under the guise of scholarship. In reality, they are adding to and taking away from God's eternal Word and upon those who do this, God has pronounced His eternal judgment.

- **Revelation 22:18** For I testify unto every man that heareth the words of the prophecy of this book, If any man shall add unto these things, God shall add unto him the plagues that are written in this book:
- **Revelation 22:19** And if any man shall take away from the words of the book of this prophecy, God shall take away his part out of the book of life, and out of the holy city, and *from* the things which are written in this book.

4. Custodians of the Faith

a. The Saints

The faithful men to whom the trust is committed, they are the salt of the earth.

- **Matthew 5:13** Ye are the salt of the earth: but if the salt have lost his savour, wherewith shall it be salted? it is thenceforth good for nothing, but to be cast out, and to be trodden under foot of men.

They must season the world with The Word of God, therefore, thy must labor above all others in defense of the truth. Otherwise they are compared to dumb dogs that bark not when the thief comes to steal away the treasure.

- **Isaiah 56:10** His watchmen *are* blind: they are all ignorant, they *are* all dumb dogs, they cannot bark; sleeping, lying down, loving to slumber.
- **Isaiah 56:11** Yea, *they are* greedy dogs *which* can never have enough, and they *are* shepherds *that* cannot understand: they all look to their own way, every one for his gain, from his quarter.

The watchman and the shepherds in Israel had given way to selfishness and debauchery. They had abandoned their responsibilities toward God's people and instead of giving warning, they were blind to the impending danger. They were dumb dogs unable to bark. Instead of watching, they were dreaming, lying down, loving to slumber.

- **John 10:10** The thief cometh not, but for to steal, and to kill, and to destroy: I am come that they might have life, and that they might have *it* more abundantly.

The words he uses are fitting pointers to the cost involved. It will be a hard difficult agonizing experience. The price is high. The test will be severe. In contending for the faith, we must guard against being contentious! We must be careful not to bring reproach to the cause of Christ, or dishonor to the Church of God. We are to speak the truth in love.

- **Ephesians 4:15** But speaking the truth in love, may grow up into him in all things, which is the head, *even* Christ:

The great need of the Church is to wake up, stand up, pray up, speak up, and be ready to go up when Jesus comes for the Church.

Chapter 4

IV. Dangerous Men – vs. 4

1. Their Entrance

a. Secret

Certain men crept in unawares. The most dangerous and subtle enemy is the one inside the Church.

- **II Peter 2:1** But there were false prophets also among the people, even as there shall be false teachers among you, who privily shall bring in damnable heresies, even denying the Lord that bought them, and bring upon themselves swift destruction.

- **I Timothy 4:1** Now the Spirit speaketh expressly, that in the latter times some shall depart from the faith, giving heed to seducing spirits, and doctrines of devils;

- **I Timothy 4:2** Speaking lies in hypocrisy; having their conscience seared with a hot iron;

- **I Timothy 4:3** Forbidding to marry, *and commanding* to abstain from meats, which God hath created to be received with thanksgiving of them which believe and know the truth.

Satan sows his tares among the wheat.

- **Matthew 13:24** Another parable put he forth unto them, saying, The kingdom of heaven is likened unto a man which sowed good seed in his field:

- **Matthew 13:25** But while men slept, his enemy came and sowed tares among the wheat, and went his way.

- **Matthew 13:26** But when the blade was sprung up, and brought forth fruit, then appeared the tares also.

- **Matthew 13:27** So the servants of the householder came and said unto him, Sir, didst not thou sow good seed in thy field? from whence then hath it tares?

- **Matthew 13:28** He said unto them, An enemy hath done this. The servants said unto him, Wilt thou then that we go and gather them up?

- **Matthew 13:29** But he said, Nay; lest while ye gather up the tares, ye root up also the wheat with them.

- **Matthew 13:30** Let both grow together until the harvest: and in the time of harvest I will say to the reapers, Gather ye together first the tares, and bind them in bundles to burn them: but gather the wheat into my barn.

He does this in the night while men slept in order to corrupt the Church. They creep in unnoticed and under false pretense. Ravening wolves in sheep's clothing

- **Matthew 7:15** Beware of false prophets, which come to you in sheep's clothing, but inwardly they are ravening wolves.

False apostles, deceitful workers, transforming

themselves into the apostles of Christ.

- **II Corinthians 11:13** For such *are* false apostles, deceitful workers, transforming themselves into the apostles of Christ.
- **II Corinthians 11:14** And no marvel; for Satan himself is transformed into an angel of light.
- **II Corinthians 11:15** Therefore *it is* no great thing if his ministers also be transformed as the ministers of righteousness; whose end shall be according to their works.

Jude says apostasy was written and condemned long ago who were before of old ordained to this condemnation. Ordained means prepared. Condemnation means judgment. "Of old" – where was it written about? Jude has the scripture in mind. Later in his letter in verse 11, he is going to cite three examples of false teachers of previous generations who troubled God's people.

2. Their Conniving

a. Sly

Conniving means to pretend not to see something wrong or evil; to help someone secretly in wrong doing; able to fool or trick others; cunning, crafty, the sly fox. This is practiced in both religion and politics.

Ungodly men turning the grace of God into lasciviousness. Lasciviousness denotes excess, absence of restraint, lewd or lustful, indecency. It describes a person so lost to dishonor, indecency, and shame he does not care who sees his sin and immorality. This is sex perversion of the most ungodly kind without fear and reverence before God. As they fall away from the knowledge of God's truth, Satan easily blinds their minds to the moral and spiritual consequences of sin. They feel they can behave any way the like and still be covered by forgiveness of God. They have twisted the grace of God into a justification for sinning. They deny The Lord God and our Lord Jesus Christ.

When a nation passes laws to protect the rights of people who are addicted to sodomy and same sex marriage to practice their perversion, society becomes partners to their excessive wickedness and is ripe for the judgment of God. What God thinks about the "alternate life-style" is abundantly clear.

- **Genesis 19:1** And there came two angels to Sodom at even; and Lot sat in the gate of Sodom: and Lot seeing *them* rose up to meet them; and he bowed himself with his face toward the ground;

- **Genesis 19:2** And he said, Behold now, my lords, turn in, I pray you, into your servant's house, and tarry all night, and wash your feet, and ye shall rise up early, and go on your ways. And they said, Nay; but we will abide in the street all night.

- **Genesis 19:3** And he pressed upon them greatly; and they turned in unto him, and entered into his house; and he made them a feast, and did bake unleavened bread, and they did eat.

- **Genesis 19:4** But before they lay down, the men of the city, *even* the men of Sodom, compassed the house round, both old and young, all the people from every quarter:

- **Genesis 19:5** And they called unto Lot, and said unto him, Where *are* the men which came in to thee this night? bring them out unto us, that we may know them.

- **Genesis 19:6** And Lot went out at the door unto them, and shut the door after him,

- **Genesis 19:7** And said, I pray you, brethren, do not so wickedly.

- **Genesis 19:8** Behold now, I have two daughters which have not known man; let me, I pray you, bring them out unto you, and do ye to them as *is* good in your eyes: only unto these men do nothing; for therefore came they under the shadow of my roof.

- **Genesis 19:9** And they said, Stand back. And they said *again,* This one *fellow* came in to sojourn, and he will needs be a judge: now will we deal worse with thee, than with them. And they pressed sore upon the man, *even* Lot, and came near to break the door.

- **Genesis 19:10** But the men put forth their hand, and pulled Lot into the house to them, and shut to the door.

- **Genesis 19:11** And they smote the men that *were* at the door of the house with blindness, both small and great: so that they wearied themselves to find the door.

- **Genesis 19:12** And the men said unto Lot, Hast thou here any besides? son in law, and thy sons, and thy daughters, and whatsoever thou hast in the city, bring *them* out of this place:

- **Genesis 19:13** For we will destroy this place, because the cry of them is waxen great before the face of the LORD; and the LORD hath sent us to destroy it.

- **Genesis 19:14** And Lot went out, and spake unto his sons in law, which married his daughters, and said, Up, get you out of this place; for the LORD will destroy this city. But he seemed as one that mocked unto his sons in law.

- **Genesis 19:15** And when the morning arose, then the angels hastened Lot, saying, Arise, take thy wife, and thy two daughters, which are here; lest thou be consumed in the iniquity of the city.

- **Genesis 19:16** And while he lingered, the men laid hold upon his hand, and upon the hand of his wife, and upon the hand of his two daughters; the LORD being merciful unto him: and they brought him forth, and set him without the city.

- **Genesis 19:17** And it came to pass, when they had brought them forth abroad, that he said, Escape for thy life; look not behind thee, neither stay thou in all the plain; escape to the mountain, lest thou be consumed.

- **Genesis 19:18** And Lot said unto them, Oh, not so, my Lord:

- **Genesis 19:19** Behold now, thy servant hath found grace in thy sight, and thou hast magnified thy mercy, which thou hast shewed unto me in saving my life; and I cannot escape to the mountain, lest some evil take me, and I die:

- **Genesis 19:20** Behold now, this city *is* near to flee unto, and it *is* a little one: Oh, let me escape thither, *(is* it not a little one?) and my soul shall live.

- **Genesis 19:21** And he said unto him, See, I have accepted thee concerning this thing also, that I will not overthrow this city, for the which thou hast spoken.

- **Genesis 19:22** Haste thee, escape thither; for I cannot do any thing till thou be come thither. Therefore the name of the city was called Zoar.

God Destroys Sodom

- **Genesis 19:23** The sun was risen upon the earth when Lot entered into Zoar.

- **Genesis 19:24** Then the LORD rained upon Sodom and upon Gomorrah brimstone and fire from the LORD out of heaven;

- **Genesis 19:25** And he overthrew those cities, and all the plain, and all the inhabitants of the cities, and that which grew upon the ground.

- **Genesis 19:26** But his wife looked back from behind him, and she became a pillar of salt.

- **Genesis 19:27** And Abraham gat up early in the morning to the place where he stood before the LORD:

- **Genesis 19:28** And he looked toward Sodom and Gomorrah, and toward all the land of the plain, and beheld, and, lo, the smoke of the country went up as the smoke of a furnace.

- **Genesis 19:29** And it came to pass, when God destroyed the cities of the plain, that God remembered Abraham, and sent Lot out of the midst of the overthrow, when he overthrew the cities in the which Lot dwelt.

Lot and His Daughters

- **Genesis 19:30** And Lot went up out of Zoar, and dwelt in the mountain, and his two daughters with him; for he feared to dwell in Zoar: and he dwelt in a cave, he and his two daughters.

- **Genesis 19:31** And the firstborn said unto the younger, Our father *is* old, and *there is* not a man in the earth to come in unto us after the manner of all the earth:

- **Genesis 19:32** Come, let us make our father drink wine, and we will lie with him, that we may preserve seed of our father.

- **Genesis 19:33** And they made their father drink wine that night: and the firstborn went in, and lay with her father; and he perceived not when she lay down, nor when she arose.

- **Genesis 19:34** And it came to pass on the morrow, that the firstborn said unto the younger, Behold, I lay yesternight with my father: let us make him drink wine this night also; and go thou in, *and* lie with him, that we may preserve seed of our father.

- **Genesis 19:35** And they made their father drink wine that night also: and the younger arose, and lay with him; and he perceived not when she lay down, nor when she arose.

- **Genesis 19:36** Thus were both the daughters of Lot with child by their father.

- **Genesis 19:37** And the firstborn bare a son, and called his name Moab: the same *is* the father of the Moabites unto this day.

- **Genesis 19:38** And the younger, she also bare a son, and called his name Benammi: the same *is* the father of the children of Ammon unto this day.

God's Word says in **Genesis 13:13** "But the men of Sodom *were* wicked and sinners before the LORD

24

exceedingly." The Hebrew word for "wickedness" means injurious, hurtful, fierce, wild. That is a description of our times today. The Hebrew word for "sinners" means meditated wickedness, plotted, planned wickedness, especially of sins of unchastity.

Chapter 5

V. Destroyed – vs. 5, 6, 7

1. A call to remembrance – vs. 5, 6, 7

- **Jude 1:5** I will therefore put you in remembrance, though ye once knew this, how that the Lord, having saved the people out of the land of Egypt, afterward destroyed them that believed not.
- **Jude 1:6** And the angels which kept not their first estate, but left their own habitation, he hath reserved in everlasting chains under darkness unto the judgment of the great day.
- **Jude 1:7** Even as Sodom and Gomorrha, and the cities about them in like manner, giving themselves over to fornication, and going after strange flesh, are set forth for an example, suffering the vengeance of eternal fire.

I will therefore put you in remembrance of verses 5 thru 7. Both call the believers to remembrance of The Word of our Lord. Human nature is prong to forgetfulness and always needs to be reminded of those things that are eternal. How easy it is to forget. Jude reminds his readers of three Old Testament groups as illustrations of warnings against turning away from God's truth in verses 5 thru 7. The nation Israel, the angels, and Sodom and Gomorrah; all have one thing in common, they fell. Israel lost its victory, the angels lost their vocation, and Sodom its virtue.

A. Remember the Israelites verses

    i. Rebellion of Israel

God miraculously delivered all the Israelites out of Egypt and destroyed those who apostatized. This is what Jude wants them to remember, not anything new about departure from the truth. It is as old as Cain in verse 11. How necessary is the daily reading of The Word.

The word "saved" means brought over the Red Sea. Three questions:

1. What was salvation?
   a. More than escape from Egypt. It was new life, new nation, even a new calendar!
2. What was unbelief?
   a. Departure from The Word of God
3. What was destruction?
   a. Destruction of the flesh that the spirit may be saved in the day of The Lord Jesus.
      - **I Corinthians 5:5** To deliver such an one unto Satan for the destruction of the flesh, that the spirit may be saved in the day of the Lord Jesus.

God only wanted their thankfulness, affections, and trust.

Their thankfulness

- **Psalm 100:4** Enter into his gates with thanksgiving, *and* into his courts with praise: be thankful unto him, *and* bless his name.
- **Colossians 3:15** And let the peace of God rule in

your hearts, to the which also ye are called in one body; and be ye thankful.

- **I Thessalonians 5:18** In every thing give thanks: for this is the will of God in Christ Jesus concerning you.

Their affections

- **Colossians 3:2** Set your affection on things above, not on things on the earth.

Their trust

- **Proverbs 3:5** Trust in the LORD with all thine heart; and lean not unto thine own understanding.
- **Proverbs 3:6** In all thy ways acknowledge him, and he shall direct thy paths.

But within a few days, they began to grumble and complain. First about food, second about water, and third, later about the leadership of Moses and Aaron. And at the first opportunity while Moses was away on Mt. Sinai receiving The Law from the very finger of God, the Israelites turn to idolatry.

- **Exodus 31:18** And he gave unto Moses, when he had made an end of communing with him upon mount Sinai, two tables of testimony, tables of stone, written with the finger of God.
- **Exodus 32:1** And when the people saw that Moses delayed to come down out of the mount, the people gathered themselves together unto Aaron, and said unto him, Up, make us gods, which shall go before us; for *as for* this Moses, the man that

brought us up out of the land of Egypt, we wot not what is become of him.

- **Exodus 32:2** And Aaron said unto them, Break off the golden earrings, which *are* in the ears of your wives, of your sons, and of your daughters, and bring *them* unto me.

- **Exodus 32:3** And all the people brake off the golden earrings which *were* in their ears, and brought *them* unto Aaron.

- **Exodus 32:4** And he received *them* at their hand, and fashioned it with a graving tool, after he had made it a molten calf: and they said, These *be* thy gods, O Israel, which brought thee up out of the land of Egypt.

- **Exodus 32:5** And when Aaron saw *it,* he built an altar before it; and Aaron made proclamation, and said, To morrow *is* a feast to the LORD.

- **Exodus 32:6** And they rose up early on the morrow, and offered burnt offerings, and brought peace offerings; and the people sat down to eat and to drink, and rose up to play.

- **Exodus 32:7** And the LORD said unto Moses, Go, get thee down; for thy people, which thou broughtest out of the land of Egypt, have corrupted *themselves:*

- **Exodus 32:8** They have turned aside quickly out of the way which I commanded them: they have made them a molten calf, and have worshipped it, and have sacrificed thereunto, and said, These *be* thy gods, O Israel, which have brought thee up out of the land of Egypt.

- **Exodus 32:9** And the LORD said unto Moses, I have seen this people, and, behold, it *is* a stiffnecked people:

- **Exodus 32:10** Now therefore let me alone, that my wrath may wax hot against them, and that I may consume them: and I will make of thee a great nation.

- **Exodus 32:11** And Moses besought the LORD his God, and said, LORD, why doth thy wrath wax hot against thy people, which thou hast brought forth out of the land of Egypt with great power, and with a mighty hand?

- **Exodus 32:12** Wherefore should the Egyptians speak, and say, For mischief did he bring them out, to slay them in the mountains, and to consume them from the face of the earth? Turn from thy fierce wrath, and repent of this evil against thy people.

- **Exodus 32:13** Remember Abraham, Isaac, and Israel, thy servants, to whom thou swarest by thine own self, and saidst unto them, I will multiply your seed as the stars of heaven, and all this land that I have spoken of will I give unto your seed, and they shall inherit *it* for ever.

- **Exodus 32:14** And the LORD repented of the evil which he thought to do unto his people.

- **Exodus 32:15** And Moses turned, and went down from the mount, and the two tables of the testimony *were* in his hand: the tables *were* written on both their sides; on the one side and on the other *were* they written.

- **Exodus 32:16** And the tables *were* the work of God, and the writing *was* the writing of God, graven upon the tables.

- **Exodus 32:17** And when Joshua heard the noise of the people as they shouted, he said unto Moses, *There is* a noise of war in the camp.

- **Exodus 32:18** And he said, *It is* not the voice of *them that* shout for mastery, neither *is it* the voice of *them that* cry for being overcome: *but* the noise of *them that* sing do I hear.

- **Exodus 32:19** And it came to pass, as soon as he came nigh unto the camp, that he saw the calf, and the dancing: and Moses' anger waxed hot, and he cast the tables out of his hands, and brake them beneath the mount.

- **Exodus 32:20** And he took the calf which they had made, and burnt *it* in the fire, and ground *it* to powder, and strawed *it* upon the water, and made the children of Israel drink *of it.*

- **Exodus 32:21** And Moses said unto Aaron, What did this people unto thee, that thou hast brought so great a sin upon them?

- **Exodus 32:22** And Aaron said, Let not the anger of my lord wax hot: thou knowest the people, that they *are set* on mischief.

- **Exodus 32:23** For they said unto me, Make us gods, which shall go before us: for *as for* this Moses, the man that brought us up out of the land of Egypt, we wot not what is become of him.

- **Exodus 32:24** And I said unto them, Whosoever hath any gold, let them break *it* off. So they gave *it* me: then I cast it into the fire, and there came out this calf.

- **Exodus 32:25** And when Moses saw that the people *were* naked; (for Aaron had made them naked unto *their* shame among their enemies:)

- **Exodus 32:26** Then Moses stood in the gate of the camp, and said, Who *is* on the LORD'S side? *let him come* unto me. And all the sons of Levi gathered themselves together unto him.

- **Exodus 32:27** And he said unto them, Thus saith the LORD God of Israel, Put every man his sword by his side, *and* go in and out from gate to gate throughout the camp, and slay every man his brother, and every man his companion, and every man his neighbour.

- **Exodus 32:28** And the children of Levi did according to the word of Moses: and there fell of the people that day about three thousand men.

- **Exodus 32:29** For Moses had said, Consecrate yourselves to day to the LORD, even every man upon his son, and upon his brother; that he may bestow upon you a blessing this day.

- **Exodus 32:30** And it came to pass on the morrow, that Moses said unto the people, Ye have sinned a great sin: and now I will go up unto the LORD; peradventure I shall make an atonement for your sin.

- **Exodus 32:31** And Moses returned unto the LORD, and said, Oh, this people have sinned a great sin, and have made them gods of gold.

- **Exodus 32:32** Yet now, if thou wilt forgive their sin; and if not, blot me, I pray thee, out of thy book which thou hast written.

- **Exodus 32:33** And the LORD said unto Moses, Whosoever hath sinned against me, him will I blot out of my book.

- **Exodus 32:34** Therefore now go, lead the people unto *the place* of which I have spoken unto thee: behold, mine Angel shall go before thee: nevertheless in the day when I visit I will visit their sin upon them.

- **Exodus 32:35** And the LORD plagued the people, because they made the calf, which Aaron made.

Jude reminds his readers that God deals severely with those who turn their backs on Him.

The Sin unto Death

I John 5:16 tells us that there is a sin unto death that believers can commit.

- **I John 5:16** If any man see his brother sin a sin *which is* not unto death, he shall ask, and he shall give him life for them that sin not unto death. There is a sin unto death: I do not say that he shall pray for it.

All sin leads to death.

- **Romans 6:23** For the wages of sin *is* death; but the gift of God *is* eternal life through Jesus Christ our Lord.

Moses and Aaron sinned unto death, however, in some cases God deems (judges) it time for a person to leave this life immediately.

- **Numbers 20:1** Then came the children of Israel, *even* the whole congregation, into the desert of Zin in the first month: and the people abode in Kadesh; and Miriam died there, and was buried there.

The Waters of Meribah

- **Numbers 20:2** And there was no water for the congregation: and they gathered themselves together against Moses and against Aaron.

- **Numbers 20:3** And the people chode with Moses, and spake, saying, Would God that we had died when our brethren died before the LORD!

- **Numbers 20:4** And why have ye brought up the congregation of the LORD into this wilderness, that we and our cattle should die there?

- **Numbers 20:5** And wherefore have ye made us to come up out of Egypt, to bring us in unto this evil place? it *is* no place of seed, or of figs, or of vines, or of pomegranates; neither *is* there any water to drink.

- **Numbers 20:6** And Moses and Aaron went from the presence of the assembly unto the door of the tabernacle of the congregation, and they fell upon their faces: and the glory of the LORD appeared unto them.

- **Numbers 20:7** And the LORD spake unto Moses, saying,

- **Numbers 20:8** Take the rod, and gather thou the assembly together, thou, and Aaron thy brother, and speak ye unto the rock before their eyes; and it shall give forth his water, and thou shalt bring forth to them water out of the rock: so thou shalt give the congregation and their beasts drink.

- **Numbers 20:9** And Moses took the rod from before the LORD, as he commanded him.

Moses Strikes the Rock

- **Numbers 20:10** And Moses and Aaron gathered the congregation together before the rock, and he said unto them, Hear now, ye rebels; must we fetch you water out of this rock?

- **Numbers 20:11** And Moses lifted up his hand, and with his rod he smote the rock twice: and the water came out abundantly, and the congregation drank, and their beasts *also.*

- **Numbers 20:12** And the LORD spake unto Moses and Aaron, Because ye believed me not, to sanctify me in the eyes of the children of Israel, therefore ye shall not bring this congregation into the land which I have given them.

- **Numbers 20:13** This *is* the water of Meribah; because the children of Israel strove with the LORD, and he was sanctified in them.

The Death of Aaron

- **Numbers 20:22** And the children of Israel, *even* the whole congregation, journeyed from Kadesh, and came unto mount Hor.

- **Numbers 20:23** And the LORD spake unto Moses and Aaron in mount Hor, by the coast of the land of Edom, saying,

- **Numbers 20:24** Aaron shall be gathered unto his people: for he shall not enter into the land which I have given unto the children of Israel, because ye rebelled against my word at the water of Meribah.

- **Numbers 20:25** Take Aaron and Eleazar his son, and bring them up unto mount Hor:

- **Numbers 20:26** And strip Aaron of his garments,

and put them upon Eleazar his son: and Aaron shall be gathered *unto his people,* and shall die there.

- **Numbers 20:27** And Moses did as the LORD commanded: and they went up into mount Hor in the sight of all the congregation.
- **Numbers 20:28** And Moses stripped Aaron of his garments, and put them upon Eleazar his son; and Aaron died there in the top of the mount: and Moses and Eleazar came down from the mount.
- **Numbers 20:29** And when all the congregation saw that Aaron was dead, they mourned for Aaron thirty days, *even* all the house of Israel.

Moses' Death Foretold

- **Deuteronomy 32:48** And the LORD spake unto Moses that selfsame day, saying,
- **Deuteronomy 32:49** Get thee up into this mountain Abarim, *unto* mount Nebo, which *is* in the land of Moab, that *is* over against Jericho; and behold the land of Canaan, which I give unto the children of Israel for a possession:
- **Deuteronomy 32:50** And die in the mount whither thou goest up, and be gathered unto thy people; as Aaron thy brother died in mount Hor, and was gathered unto his people:
- **Deuteronomy 32:51** Because ye trespassed against me among the children of Israel at the waters of Meribah-Kadesh, in the wilderness of Zin; because ye sanctified me not in the midst of the children of Israel.
- **Deuteronomy 32:52** Yet thou shalt see the land

before *thee;* but thou shalt not go thither unto the land which I give the children of Israel.

Ananias and Sapphira are perfect examples of the sin unto death.

- **Acts 5:1** But a certain man named Ananias, with Sapphira his wife, sold a possession,
- **Acts 5:2** And kept back *part* of the price, his wife also being privy *to it,* and brought a certain part, and laid *it* at the apostles' feet.
- **Acts 5:3** But Peter said, Ananias, why hath Satan filled thine heart to lie to the Holy Ghost, and to keep back *part* of the price of the land?
- **Acts 5:4** Whiles it remained, was it not thine own? and after it was sold, was it not in thine own power? why hast thou conceived this thing in thine heart? thou hast not lied unto men, but unto God.
- **Acts 5:5** And Ananias hearing these words fell down, and gave up the ghost: and great fear came on all them that heard these things.
- **Acts 5:6** And the young men arose, wound him up, and carried *him* out, and buried *him.*
- **Acts 5:7** And it was about the space of three hours after, when his wife, not knowing what was done, came in.
- **Acts 5:8** And Peter answered unto her, Tell me whether ye sold the land for so much? And she said, Yea, for so much.
- **Acts 5:9** Then Peter said unto her, How is it that ye have agreed together to tempt the Spirit of the Lord? behold, the feet of them which have buried thy

husband *are* at the door, and shall carry thee out.

- **Acts 5:10** Then fell she down straightway at his feet, and yielded up the ghost: and the young men came in, and found her dead, and, carrying *her* forth, buried *her* by her husband.
- **Acts 5:11** And great fear came upon all the church, and upon as many as heard these things.

The Corinthians abused The Lord's supper. Many were weak (feeble) and sickly and many sleep, that is died

- **I Corinthians 11:30** For this cause many *are* weak and sickly among you, and many sleep.

The sin unto death is not a single act but a continual habit.

2. Recognition

Jude reminds us how they once knew how the Lord saved the people out of the land of Egypt and destroyed them that did not believe.

- **Jude 1:5** … though ye once knew this, how that the Lord, having saved the people out of the land of Egypt, afterward destroyed them that believed not.

The word "knew" means to discern clearly. The greater the light, the greater the accountability.

3. Retribution

The Lord destroyed them that did not believe. Their unbelief destroyed their witness, their testimony, their joy, their reward, their victory, and their physical life. Although their soul will not be lost.

- **I Corinthians 5:5** To deliver such an one unto Satan for the destruction of the flesh, that the spirit may be saved in the day of the Lord Jesus.

B. Remember the angels that sinned

- **Jude 1:6** And the angels which kept not their first estate, but left their own habitation, he hath reserved in everlasting chains under darkness unto the judgment of the great day.

    i. Disobedient angels

There are two subdivisions of angels

1. The Fallen Free Angels

The fallen free angels dwell with Satan in the first heaven above the earth. In Ephesians 2:2, Satan is called the prince of the power of the air. The fallen angels are under the control of Satan. They are free to roam the earth to do Satan's evil work. Satan is not omnipresent. He cannot be present everywhere at the same time. So Satan instructs his angels to do his bidding.

- **Ephesians 2:2** Wherein in time past ye walked according to the course of this world, according to the prince of the power of the air, the spirit that now worketh in the children of disobedience:

2. The Fallen Confined Angels

The sin of these angels was fornication by cohabitating with the women described in Genesis 6:1-4 and Jude 6-7.

- **Genesis 6:1** And it came to pass, when men began to multiply on the face of the earth, and daughters were born unto them,
- **Genesis 6:2** That the sons of God saw the daughters of men that they *were* fair; and they took them wives of all which they chose.
- **Genesis 6:3** And the LORD said, My spirit shall not always strive with man, for that he also *is* flesh: yet his days shall be an hundred and twenty years.
- **Genesis 6:4** There were giants in the earth in those days; and also after that, when the sons of God came in unto the daughters of men, and they bare *children* to them, the same *became* mighty men which *were* of old, men of renown.

- **Jude 1:6** And the angels which kept not their first estate, but left their own habitation, he hath reserved in everlasting chains under darkness unto the judgment of the great day.
- **Jude 1:7** Even as Sodom and Gomorrha, and the cities about them in like manner, giving themselves over to fornication, and going after strange flesh, are set forth for an example, suffering the vengeance of eternal fire.

Their sin was so gross and abominable against nature

that God cast these angels down to hell.

- **II Peter 2:4** For if God spared not the angels that sinned, but cast *them* down to hell, and delivered *them* into chains of darkness, to be reserved unto judgment;

Here hell is translated "Tartarus" which means "bottomless pit". Literally, the "abyss" which means "unfathomably deep". Peter is speaking of that place in the unseen underworld where the fallen angels are incarcerated until the great white throne judgement.

Judgment Before the Great White Throne

- **Revelation 20:11** And I saw a great white throne, and him that sat on it, from whose face the earth and the heaven fled away; and there was found no place for them.

- **Revelation 20:12** And I saw the dead, small and great, stand before God; and the books were opened: and another book was opened, which is *the book* of life: and the dead were judged out of those things which were written in the books, according to their works.

- **Revelation 20:13** And the sea gave up the dead which were in it; and death and hell delivered up the dead which were in them: and they were judged every man according to their works.

- **Revelation 20:14** And death and hell were cast into the lake of fire. This is the second death.

- **Revelation 20:15** And whosoever was not found written in the book of life was cast into the lake of fire.

3. The Failure of the Fallen Angels

- **Jude 1:6** And the angels which kept not their first estate, but left their own habitation, he hath reserved in everlasting chains under darkness unto the judgment of the great day.

"Kept not" is the aorist tense and denotes to guard, to watch, to keep. These angels did not fulfill their obligation of watching and guarding their original position.

"First estate" means dominion. These angels did not remain in the domain that God intended for angels. They left it to become part of domain that God had not ordained for angels.

"Left" is the aorist tense and means to leave behind, a once for all act. These angels abandoned heaven and left forever. You could say they burnt their bridges.

"Habitation" means a dwelling place and here that place is heaven.

"Reserved" means to keep, guard, under guard continually.

"Darkness" here this is a thick darkness; a darkness that may be felt. Their prison is escape proof. No prospect of restoration awaits them. Their fall is final.

"Angels" means messenger. God has heavenly messengers but the word angel is also translated as a human messenger. John the Baptist is an example of this.

- **Matthew 11:10** For this is *he,* of whom it is written, Behold, I send my messenger before thy face, which shall prepare thy way before thee.

Angels are always spoken of in the masculine gender.

- **Daniel 9:21** Yea, whiles I *was* speaking in prayer, even the man Gabriel, whom I had seen in the vision at the beginning, being caused to fly swiftly, touched me about the time of the evening oblation.

- **Mark 16:5** And entering into the sepulchre, they saw a young man sitting on the right side, clothed in a long white garment; and they were affrighted.

- **Luke 24:4** And it came to pass, as they were much perplexed thereabout, behold, two men stood by them in shining garments:

Thus they appear to have the power of materializing and assuming the functions of a human body. In Genesis 18:1-8 the Lord and two angels appeared to Abraham. Abraham, Sarah, and a young man prepared them a meal and they did eat.

- **Genesis 18:1** And the LORD appeared unto him in the plains of Mamre: and he sat in the tent door in the heat of the day;
- **Genesis 18:2** And he lift up his eyes and looked, and, lo, three men stood by him: and when he saw *them,* he ran to meet them from the tent door, and bowed himself toward the ground,

- **Genesis 18:3** And said, My Lord, if now I have found favour in thy sight, pass not away, I pray thee, from thy servant:

- **Genesis 18:4** Let a little water, I pray you, be fetched, and wash your feet, and rest yourselves under the tree:

- **Genesis 18:5** And I will fetch a morsel of bread, and comfort ye your hearts; after that ye shall pass on: for therefore are ye come to your servant. And they said, So do, as thou hast said.

- **Genesis 18:6** And Abraham hastened into the tent unto Sarah, and said, Make ready quickly three measures of fine meal, knead *it,* and make cakes upon the hearth.

- **Genesis 18:7** And Abraham ran unto the herd, and fetcht a calf tender and good, and gave *it* unto a young man; and he hasted to dress it.

- **Genesis 18:8** And he took butter, and milk, and the calf which he had dressed, and set *it* before them; and he stood by them under the tree, and they did eat.

In Genesis 19:3 they eat Lot's unleavened bread. Those were holy angels and their mission was to destroy Sodom and Gomorrah.

- **Genesis 19:3** And he pressed upon them greatly; and they turned in unto him, and entered into his house; and he made them a feast, and did bake unleavened bread, and they did eat.

If the holy angels have power to materialize and assume

the functions of a human body, I believe the fallen angels had the same power when they cohabitated with the women in Genesis 6:1-4. Their offspring was giants which means "fallen ones"; a direct reference to the fallen angels who fathered them.

- **Genesis 6:1** And it came to pass, when men began to multiply on the face of the earth, and daughters were born unto them,

- **Genesis 6:2** That the sons of God saw the daughters of men that they *were* fair; and they took them wives of all which they chose.

- **Genesis 6:3** And the LORD said, My spirit shall not always strive with man, for that he also *is* flesh: yet his days shall be an hundred and twenty years.

- **Genesis 6:4** There were giants in the earth in those days; and also after that, when the sons of God came in unto the daughters of men, and they bare *children* to them, the same *became* mighty men which *were* of old, men of renown.

It was Satan's purpose to contaminate the whole Adamic womanhood, and thereby to prevent the advent of the promised seed; the seed of the woman, the birth of Jesus Christ.

- **Genesis 3:15** And I will put enmity between thee and the woman, and between thy seed and her seed; it shall bruise thy head, and thou shalt bruise his heel.

- **Matthew 1:18** Now the birth of Jesus Christ was on this wise: When as his mother Mary was espoused to Joseph, before they came together, she was found with child of the Holy Ghost.

- **Matthew 1:19** Then Joseph her husband, being a just *man,* and not willing to make her a publick example, was minded to put her away privily.

- **Matthew 1:20** But while he thought on these things, behold, the angel of the Lord appeared unto him in a dream, saying, Joseph, thou son of David, fear not to take unto thee Mary thy wife: for that which is conceived in her is of the Holy Ghost.

- **Matthew 1:21** And she shall bring forth a son, and thou shalt call his name JESUS: for he shall save his people from their sins.

- **Matthew 1:22** Now all this was done, that it might be fulfilled which was spoken of the Lord by the prophet, saying,

- **Matthew 1:23** Behold, a virgin shall be with child, and shall bring forth a son, and they shall call his name Emmanuel, which being interpreted is, God with us.

- **Matthew 1:24** Then Joseph being raised from sleep did as the angel of the Lord had bidden him, and took unto him his wife:

- **Matthew 1:25** And knew her not till she had brought forth her firstborn son: and he called his name JESUS.

- **Luke 2:1** And it came to pass in those days, that there went out a decree from Caesar Augustus, that all the world should be taxed.

- **Luke 2:2** *(And* this taxing was first made when Cyrenius was governor of Syria.)

- **Luke 2:3** And all went to be taxed, every one into his own city.

- **Luke 2:4** And Joseph also went up from Galilee,

out of the city of Nazareth, into Judaea, unto the city of David, which is called Bethlehem; (because he was of the house and lineage of David:)

- **Luke 2:5** To be taxed with Mary his espoused wife, being great with child.

- **Luke 2:6** And so it was, that, while they were there, the days were accomplished that she should be delivered.

- **Luke 2:7** And she brought forth her firstborn son, and wrapped him in swaddling clothes, and laid him in a manger; because there was no room for them in the inn.

I believe the chronological order supports this view.

    a. The angels that sinned

- **II Peter 2:4** For if God spared not the angels that sinned, but cast *them* down to hell, and delivered *them* into chains of darkness, to be reserved unto judgment;

    b. Noah's flood

- **II Peter 2:5** And spared not the old world, but saved Noah the eighth *person,* a preacher of righteousness, bringing in the flood upon the world of the ungodly;

    c. Sodom and Gomorrah

- **II Peter 2:6** And turning the cities of Sodom and Gomorrha into ashes condemned *them* with an overthrow, making *them* an ensample unto those that after should live ungodly;

Judgement of the angels is mentioned in verse 4 just before the judgement of the world by the flood in verse 5. This fits the chronology in Genesis 6:1-4.

The term "sons of God" in Genesis 6:2 is only found three other times in the Old Testament.

- **Job 1:6** Now there was a day when the sons of God came to present themselves before the LORD, and Satan came also among them.

- **Job 2:1** Again there was a day when the sons of God came to present themselves before the LORD, and Satan came also among them to present himself before the LORD.

- **Job 38:7** When the morning stars sang together, and all the sons of God shouted for joy?

The fallen angels went beyond their limitations and a forbidden sexual barrier God had appointed. The objection to this interpretation in Genesis 6:1-4 is that Jesus taught that in the resurrection they neither marry, nor are given in marriage, but are as the angels of God in heaven.

- **Matthew 22:30** For in the resurrection they neither marry, nor are given in marriage, but are as the angels of God in heaven.

True, but Jesus was speaking of the holy angels who remained in heaven under God's dominion. He was not speaking about fallen angels who had left their habitation in heaven.

Although this biblical revelation may be difficult for the modern mind, the literal interpretation of these aforementioned scriptures gives much weight to this interpretation.

Each angel is a direct creation of God. Therefore they are called the sons of God in Genesis 6:2, Job 1:6, Job 2:1, and Job 38:7.

i.   The Sons of God in three categories

The companion Bible in appendixes 23 states that it is only by divine specific act of creation that any created being can be called a "son of God".

1.   The Angels are a divine specific creation of God

Bible scholars disagree concerning the interpretation of Genesis 6:2.

- **Genesis 6:2** That the sons of God saw the daughters of men that they *were* fair; and they took them wives of all which they chose.

Some say the sons of God refers to the Godly lineage of Seth. Since the designation "sons of God" is consistently used in the Old testament for angels, it is logical to conclude that the term in Genesis 6:2 refers to angels. Gesenius' Hebrew-Chaldee Lexicon on the Old Testament says Genesis 6:2 means angels.

2. Adam was a divine specific creation of God

Adam was specifically created by God.

- **Genesis 5:1** This *is* the book of the generations of Adam. In the day that God created man, in the likeness of God made he him;

- **Genesis 1:27** So God created man in his *own* image, in the image of God created he him; male and female created he them.

This explains why Adam is called a son of God in Luke 3:38.

- **Luke 3:38** Which was *the son* of Enos, which was *the son* of Seth, which was *the son* of Adam, which was *the son* of God.

However, Adams' descendants are different. They were not in God's likeness, but in Adam's. Adam begat a son in his own likeness, after his image.

- **Genesis 5:3** And Adam lived an hundred and thirty years, and begat *a son* in his own likeness, after his image; and called his name Seth:

Adam was a "son of God" but Adam's descendants were "sons of men".

3. Born again believers are a divine specific creation of God

- **II Corinthians 5:17** Therefore if any man *be* in Christ, *he is* a new creature: old things are passed away; behold, all things are become new.

"Creature" means creation.

- **John 1:12** But as many as received him, to them gave he power to become the sons of God, *even* to them that believe on his name:

"As many" means no matter whether they be male or female, young or old, poor or rich, Jew or Gentile, illiterate or intellectual, all must confess they are sinners in need of a Savior.

- **Romans 10:8** But what saith it? The word is nigh thee, *even* in thy mouth, and in thy heart: that is, the word of faith, which we preach;

- **Romans 10:9** That if thou shalt confess with thy mouth the Lord Jesus, and shalt believe in thine heart that God hath raised him from the dead, thou shalt be saved.

- **Romans 10:13** For whosoever shall call upon the name of the Lord shall be saved.

- **Revelation 22:17** ... And let him that is athirst come. And whosoever will, let him take the water of life freely.

Chapter 6

VI. Remember Sodom and Gomorrah - vs. 7

ii.   Defiled Citizens

- **Jude 1:7** Even as Sodom and Gomorrha, and the cities about them in like manner, giving themselves over to fornication, and going after strange flesh, are set forth for an example, suffering the vengeance of eternal fire.

The sins that caused the fall of Sodom and Gomorrah is that which will cause the fall of the United States of America.

- **Ezekiel 16:49** Behold, this was the iniquity of thy sister Sodom, pride, fulness of bread, and abundance of idleness was in her and in her daughters, neither did she strengthen the hand of the poor and needy.

1. Pride

- **Proverbs 16:18** Pride *goeth* before destruction, and an haughty spirit before a fall.

- **Ezekiel 16:50** And they were haughty, and committed abomination before me: therefore I took them away as I saw *good.*

Unbelief is a great sin, but the hidden germ of that sin is pride.

2. Fulness of Bread

Sodom had satisfaction in her prosperity and abundance of food. She monopolized the blessings for her own pleasures and basked in prosperous ease.

This is a false security for a man's life does not consist in the abundance of the things which he has.

- **Luke 12:15** And he said unto them, Take heed, and beware of covetousness: for a man's life consisteth not in the abundance of the things which he possesseth.

3. Abundance of idleness

They had too much leisure time. It has been said that idleness is the devil's workshop.

4. Indifference to the poor and needy

Selfishness will neglect the poor.

- **Proverbs 21:13** Whoso stoppeth his ears at the cry of the poor, he also shall cry himself, but shall not be heard.
- **Psalm 41:1 To the chief Musician, A Psalm of**

David. Blessed *is* he that considereth the poor: the LORD will deliver him in time of trouble.

- **Proverbs 19:17** He that hath pity upon the poor lendeth unto the LORD; and that which he hath given will he pay him again.

Paul was unselfish and ministered to the poor.

- **Galatians 2:10** Only *they would* that we should remember the poor; the same which I also was forward to do.

5. Homosexuality

Sodom and Gomorrah and the cities about them were well known for their horrid sexual perversion. Today it is often referred to as "sodomy".

This is not a matter to be presented as unimportant or pursued lightly.

- **Romans 1:24** Wherefore God also gave them up to uncleanness through the lusts of their own hearts, to dishonour their own bodies between themselves:
- **Romans 1:25** Who changed the truth of God into a lie, and worshipped and served the creature more than the Creator, who is blessed for ever. Amen.
- **Romans 1:26** For this cause God gave them up

unto vile affections: for even their women did change the natural use into that which is against nature:

- **Romans 1:27** And likewise also the men, leaving the natural use of the woman, burned in their lust one toward another; men with men working that which is unseemly, and receiving in themselves that recompence of their error which was meet.

- **Romans 1:28** And even as they did not like to retain God in *their* knowledge, God gave them over to a reprobate mind, to do those things which are not convenient;

- **Romans 1:29** Being filled with all unrighteousness, fornication, wickedness, covetousness, maliciousness; full of envy, murder, debate, deceit, malignity; whisperers,

- **Romans 1:30** Backbiters, haters of God, despiteful, proud, boasters, inventors of evil things, disobedient to parents,

- **Romans 1:31** Without understanding, covenantbreakers, without natural affection, implacable, unmerciful:

- **Romans 1:32** Who knowing the judgment of God, that they which commit such things are worthy of death, not only do the same, but have pleasure in them that do them.

Jude's third example of Divine judgement points to the destruction of Sodom and Gomorrah and the cities about them.

- **Deuteronomy 29:23** *And that* the whole land thereof *is* brimstone, and salt, *and* burning, *that* it is not sown, nor beareth, nor any grass groweth therein, like the overthrow of Sodom, and Gomorrah, Admah, and Zeboim, which the LORD overthrew in his anger, and in his wrath:

- **Genesis 19:24** Then the LORD rained upon Sodom and upon Gomorrah brimstone and fire from the LORD out of heaven;
- **Genesis 19:25** And he overthrew those cities, and all the plain, and all the inhabitants of the cities, and that which grew upon the ground.

Jude is careful with the language used. He does not say "in the same manner as the angels", but, "in like manner" meaning in similar manner. There is a difference.

- **Jude 1:7** Even as Sodom and Gomorrha, and the cities about them in like manner, giving themselves over to fornication, and going after strange flesh, are set forth for an example, suffering the vengeance of eternal fire.

"Similar" implies partial identity, not complete identity. The sin was "like" that of the angels in that it was concerned with sex. This is the similarity, but there was a difference. The sin of the angels was fornication. The sin of the cities of Sodom and Gomorrah was homosexuality

- **Romans 1:27** And likewise also the men, leaving the natural use of the woman, burned in their lust one toward another; men with men working that which is unseemly, and receiving in themselves that recompence of their error which was meet.

Giving themselves over to fornication refers back to the angels in verse 6.

- **Genesis 6:1** And it came to pass, when men began to multiply on the face of the earth, and daughters were born unto them,
- **Genesis 6:2** That the sons of God saw the daughters of men that they *were* fair; and they took them wives of all which they chose.
- **Genesis 6:3** And the LORD said, My spirit shall not always strive with man, for that he also *is* flesh: yet his days shall be an hundred and twenty years.
- **Genesis 6:4** There were giants in the earth in those days; and also after that, when the sons of God came in unto the daughters of men, and they bare *children* to them, the same *became* mighty men which *were* of old, men of renown.

Strange flesh means another of a different kind or to indulge in unnatural lust. Angels went after flesh that God intended to be foreign to them. The fallen angels sin was cohabiting with the women before the flood as stated in Genesis 6:1-4. In verse 2, the "sons of God" means angels. Jude states in verse 7 their destiny is eternal fire.

Sodom and Gomorrah and the cities sin was homosexuality, "men with men" and their destiny will be eternal fire.

- **Romans 1:27** And likewise also the men, leaving the natural use of the woman, burned in their lust one toward another; men with men working that which is unseemly, and receiving in themselves that recompence of their error which was meet.

- **Jude 1:7** Even as Sodom and Gomorrha, and the cities about them in like manner, giving themselves over to fornication, and going after strange flesh, are set forth for an example, suffering the vengeance of eternal fire.

Can homosexuals be saved?

In Romans 1:24-28, two times the scripture says "and God gave them up" and one time "God gave them over".

- **Romans 1:24** Wherefore God also gave them up to uncleanness through the lusts of their own hearts, to dishonour their own bodies between themselves:
- **Romans 1:25** Who changed the truth of God into a lie, and worshipped and served the creature more than the Creator, who is blessed for ever. Amen.
- **Romans 1:26** For this cause God gave them up unto vile affections: for even their women did change the natural use into that which is against nature:
- **Romans 1:27** And likewise also the men, leaving the natural use of the woman, burned in their lust one toward another; men with men working that which is unseemly, and receiving in themselves that recompence of their error which was meet.
- **Romans 1:28** And even as they did not like to retain God in *their* knowledge, God gave them over

to a reprobate mind, to do those things which are not convenient;

1. God also gave them up to uncleanness

This refers to living in impurity of lust, profligate living, unclean in thought and life.

2. God gave them up unto vile affections

Vile means shame or disgrace. Vile affections are shameful, disgraceful, evil desires.

I believe those who are in the state of those described in verses 24 and 26 can be saved. Let us look at I Corinthians 6:9-11.

- **I Corinthians 6:9** Know ye not that the unrighteous shall not inherit the kingdom of God? Be not deceived: neither fornicators, nor idolaters, nor adulterers, nor effeminate, nor abusers of themselves with mankind,
- **I Corinthians 6:10** Nor thieves, nor covetous, nor drunkards, nor revilers, nor extortioners, shall inherit the kingdom of God.
- **I Corinthians 6:11** And such were some of you: but ye are washed, but ye are sanctified, but ye are justified in the name of the Lord Jesus, and by the Spirit of our God.

Paul lists ten classes of sinners. Fornicators, idolaters, adulterers, effeminate, abusers of themselves with mankind, thieves, covetous, drunkards, revilers, and extortioners. I won't comment on all of these characteristics, but I call your attention to verses 9-11.

In verse 9, the "effeminate" means homosexual males which is a description of who they are. Their conduct is they are abusers of themselves with mankind, which is a sodomite. "Abusers" refers to their immoral acts.

Look at I Corinthians 6:11 closely.

"And such were some of you". It does not say all of you. But it say "were" which means before their new birth, some of the Christians had been guilty of the sins listed in verses 9-10.

"But now ye are washed" which refers to the cleansing of regeneration.

- **Ezekiel 36:25** Then will I sprinkle clean water upon you, and ye shall be clean: from all your filthiness, and from all your idols, will I cleanse you.

- **John 3:5** Jesus answered, Verily, verily, I say unto thee, Except a man be born of water and *of* the Spirit, he cannot enter into the kingdom of God.

- **Titus 3:5** Not by works of righteousness which we have done, but according to his mercy he saved us, by the washing of regeneration, and renewing of the Holy Ghost;

"But ye are sanctified" refers to positional sanctification which is the act of God whereby the believing sinner is forever set apart from the world unto God.

"But ye are justified" refers to the act of God whereby He declares righteous that sinner who has been made righteous through faith in Jesus Christ.

"And by the Spirit of our God" refers to some of the Corinthians who had been living in immoral sins just mentioned but they are no more because they have been converted and radically changed by the blood of Jesus Christ.

- **I John 1:7** But if we walk in the light, as he is in the light, we have fellowship one with another, and the blood of Jesus Christ his Son cleanseth us from all sin.

3. God gave them over to a reprobate mind

Now going back to Romans 1:28 God gave them over to a reprobate mind. Even as they did not like to retain God in their knowledge, men did not recognize the Creator in his own world. And so with the Redeemer.

- **John 1:10** He was in the world, and the world was made by him, and the world knew him not.

God is to be retained in our knowledge. However that knowledge may be lost.

"Reprobate" means undiscerning, void of right judgment, unable to distinguish and approve what is good and right. A "reprobate mind" is a mind of which God cannot approve, and which must be rejected by Him.

- **Isaiah 5:20** Woe unto them that call evil good, and good evil; that put darkness for light, and light for darkness; that put bitter for sweet, and sweet for bitter!

- **Isaiah 44:20** He feedeth on ashes: a deceived heart hath turned him aside, that he cannot deliver his soul, nor say, *Is there* not a lie in my right hand?

"To do those things which are not convenient" means unfitting, not proper, morally wrong, forbidden, and shameful. They have abandoned God, therefore, He is left with no choice but to abandon such men to judgment and hell.

4. They banish God from their morals

- **Romans 1:29** Being filled with all unrighteousness, fornication, wickedness, covetousness, maliciousness; full of envy, murder, debate, deceit, malignity; whisperers,
- **Romans 1:30** Backbiters, haters of God, despiteful, proud, boasters, inventors of evil things, disobedient to parents,
- **Romans 1:31** Without understanding, covenantbreakers, without natural affection, implacable, unmerciful:

- **Romans 1:32** Who knowing the judgment of God, that they which commit such things are worthy of death, not only do the same, but have pleasure in them that do them.

They are governed by a reprobate mind. When sinners reach the reprobate stage, their destiny is sealed.

Chapter 7

VII. *Filthy Dreamers – vs. 8*

- **Jude 1:8** Likewise also these *filthy* dreamers defile the flesh, despise dominion, and speak evil of dignities.

Jude calls them filthy dreamers. He names three things they do.

1. Defile the Flesh

The apostle Peter wrote about the same subject and the same class of people; false prophets and false teachers.

- **II Peter 2:1** But there were false prophets also among the people, even as there shall be false teachers among you, who privily shall bring in damnable heresies, even denying the Lord that bought them, and bring upon themselves swift destruction.

- **II Peter 2:10** But chiefly them that walk after the flesh in the lust of uncleanness, and despise government. Presumptuous *are they,* selfwilled, they are not afraid to speak evil of dignities.

The idea expressed by both Peter and Jude is the sin of licentiousness. Each writer has the sin of immorality in view.

2. Despise Dominion

"Despise" means to do away with something laid down, prescribed, or established.

"Dominion" means one who possess dominion. This is a word that is also translated "lord" and speaks of one who is lord over another. It can be rendered "government". This sort of apostasy mentioned here disregards and seeks to overthrow government. Thus, these men who creep into Churches unaware are ungodly men who try to do away with The Word of God as established by inspiration and they do so by denying the only Lord God and our Savior, Jesus Christ.

3. Speak Evil of Dignities

"Speak evil" means to speak reproachfully of, rail at, revile, blaspheme, slander.

"Dignities" means splendor, brightness, preeminence.

Thus, these false teachers speak reproachfully of God's splendor and preeminence.

Chapter 8

VIII. The Dispute over Moses' Body – vs. 9

- **Jude 1:9** Yet Michael the archangel, when contending with the devil he disputed about the body of Moses, durst not bring against him a railing accusation, but said, The Lord rebuke thee.

The name Michael means "who is like God". Michael was a reflector of the glory and beauty of God. He became like the company he kept.

God's people ought to be like Him in our mind, our motives, our movements, our manners, and our ministry.

Michael is the great prince who protects Israel in the book of Daniel.

- **Daniel 12:1** And at that time shall Michael stand up, the great prince which standeth for the children of thy people: and there shall be a time of trouble, such as never was since there was a nation *even* to that same time: and at that time thy people shall be delivered, every one that shall be found written in the book.

1. The Ministry Contending

In verse 9 of Jude, Michael the archangel is contending with Satan for the body of Moses. Why did Satan want the body of Moses? John Calvin said it is beyond controversy that Moses died and was buried by The Lord and his grave concealed according to the purpose of God that neither he nor his grave become and object of worship and idolatry.

- **Deuteronomy 34:1** And Moses went up from the plains of Moab unto the mountain of Nebo, to the top of Pisgah, that *is* over against Jericho. And the LORD shewed him all the land of Gilead, unto Dan,
- **Deuteronomy 34:2** And all Naphtali, and the land of Ephraim, and Manasseh, and all the land of Judah, unto the utmost sea,
- **Deuteronomy 34:3** And the south, and the plain of the valley of Jericho, the city of palm trees, unto Zoar.
- **Deuteronomy 34:4** And the LORD said unto him, This *is* the land which I sware unto Abraham, unto Isaac, and unto Jacob, saying, I will give it unto thy seed: I have caused thee to see *it* with thine eyes, but thou shalt not go over thither.
- **Deuteronomy 34:5** So Moses the servant of the LORD died there in the land of Moab, according to the word of the LORD.
- **Deuteronomy 34:6** And he buried him in a valley in the land of Moab, over against Bethpeor: but no man knoweth of his sepulchre unto this day.

2. The Message

- **Jude 1:9** Yet Michael the archangel, when contending with the devil he disputed about the body of Moses, durst not bring against him a railing accusation, but said, The Lord rebuke thee.

Michael doesn't bring a failing accusation against the devil. He dared not to bring this accusation against the devil.

"Rail" means to revile or scold in harsh or abusive language. God's Word is more powerful than any mental or intellectual ability that we have. It would have been inconsistent with angelical perfection to rail against the devil. There is no cowardice in Michael not daring to sin. And what was wrong for angels cannot be right for men to do. Michael left the decision absolutely in God's hands. "The Lord rebuke thee".

Chapter 9

IX.   *Debasing Behavior – vs. 10*

- **Jude 1:10** But these speak evil of those things which they know not: but what they know naturally, as brute beasts, in those things they corrupt themselves.
  - Living on the level of animals

These men who regard themselves as superior were actually on the level of animals. Jude says they speak "what they know naturally" or by instinct. Animals have instinct and act upon instinct rather than reasoning. Jude is not classifying man as an animal, but classifying their teaching as by instinct like an animal acts by instinct.

The precious doctrines of the Bible are being denied and debased today because they cannot be understood by the instinct of man. They are being destroyed by their own religion. What a pity when a man's own religion destroys him.

- **I Corinthians 2:14** But the natural man receiveth not the things of the Spirit of God: for they are foolishness unto him: neither can he know *them,* because they are spiritually discerned.

The doctrine of blood redemption cannot be understood by instinct of man

Chapter 10

X. Descriptive Pictures – vs. 11

- **Jude 1:11** Woe unto them! for they have gone in the way of Cain, and ran greedily after the error of Balaam for reward, and perished in the gainsaying of Core.

1. The Way of Cain

The way of Cain is basically the rejection of salvation through the blood of Jesus Christ. Cain refused to bring God's required sacrifice by eliminating the shed blood.

- **Genesis 4:1** And Adam knew Eve his wife; and she conceived, and bare Cain, and said, I have gotten a man from the LORD.
- **Genesis 4:2** And she again bare his brother Abel. And Abel was a keeper of sheep, but Cain was a tiller of the ground.
- **Genesis 4:3** And in process of time it came to pass, that Cain brought of the fruit of the ground an offering unto the LORD.
- **Genesis 4:4** And Abel, he also brought of the firstlings of his flock and of the fat thereof. And the LORD had respect unto Abel and to his offering:
- **Genesis 4:5** But unto Cain and to his offering he had not respect. And Cain was very wroth, and his countenance fell.

A key to the evaluating of any teacher today may be found in his attitude toward the efficacy of the blood of Jesus Christ to deal with man's sin. If he does not hold to the Bible view, he is a false teacher no matter how appealing his approach may be.

2. The Error of Balaam

Balaam's error or sin was greed for gold. He was hired by Balak for pay in order to put a curse on God's people. He knew he was not supposed to do that. He turned against God's Word and his own conscience and "sold his soul" to sin for earthy riches. In the end he was put to death.

- **Joshua 13:22** Balaam also the son of Beor, the soothsayer, did the children of Israel slay with the sword among them that were slain by them.

What shall it profit a man if he gains the whole world and loses his soul? Many today are turning away from eternal riches of God to grasp uncertain, fleeting riches of this poor world, which will pass away.

3. The Gainsaying of Core

- ❖ Spelled Core in the New Testament and Korah in the Old Testament

Korah was a cousin to Aaron and Moses.

The Genealogy of Moses and Aaron

- **Exodus 6:18** And the sons of Kohath; Amram, and Izhar, and Hebron, and Uzziel: and the years of the life of Kohath *were* an hundred thirty and three years.

- **Exodus 6:19** And the sons of Merari; Mahali and Mushi: these *are* the families of Levi according to their generations.

- **Exodus 6:20** And Amram took him Jochebed his father's sister to wife; and she bare him Aaron and Moses: and the years of the life of Amram *were* an hundred and thirty and seven years.

- **Exodus 6:21** And the sons of Izhar; Korah, and Nepheg, and Zichri.

The scriptures say a man's foes shall be of his own household.

- **Matthew 10:36** And a man's foes *shall be* they of his own household.

We cannot allow even the closes relative to come between us the Lord.

Under the cloak of standing for equality among God's people, Korah questioned the leadership of Moses and Aaron: Aren't all of the people holy? What are you doing telling us what God wants? He encouraged the Levites to complain so why can't we be priests? Why can't we do what you and Aaron do?

The services of priesthood were very definitely confined to the house of Aaron.

- **Exodus 28:1** And take thou unto thee Aaron thy brother, and his sons with him, from among the children of Israel, that he may minister unto me in the priest's office, *even* Aaron, Nadab and Abihu, Eleazar and Ithamar, Aaron's sons.

Consecration of Aaron and His Sons

- **Leviticus 8:36** So Aaron and his sons did all things which the LORD commanded by the hand of Moses.

Korah provoked discontent and it would seem he actually desired that leadership for himself. His rebellion was prompted by the idea that leadership among God's people is something to which we can appoint ourselves. This is not true. It is God who chooses leaders, gifting them, and anointing them.

There have always been self-opinionated trouble makes among God's people and in churches. Often some young man in a hurry to make it to what they see as "the top" in Christian circles becomes motivated by jealousy, by lusting after a position, and a desire to be seen. They are frequently opportunists who capitalize on difficult times to undermine God's appointed leaders who are solid experienced Christians and have led well. They will come up with these new up starts and they start casting aspersions: "old fashioned", "yesterday's men", "bad decision, "self-appointed", "let the young people lead".

But sometimes, older leaders can be too keen to hold onto their office and refuse to make way for a younger generation and this too is wrong. However, a God appointed upcoming leader will find a gracious way of coping with that situation. He will not follow Korah's rebellion.

Beware of troublemakers like Korah. Identify them and reject them. "Gainsaying" means to say against, to oppose in word and deed, to rebel.

How did Korah's sin affect his family? They perished with him when the ground opened up and swallowed them.

- **Numbers 16:32** And the earth opened her mouth, and swallowed them up, and their houses, and all the men that *appertained* unto Korah, and all *their* goods.
- **Numbers 16:33** They, and all that *appertained* to them, went down alive into the pit, and the earth closed upon them: and they perished from among the congregation.

But, there was one exception as recorded in Numbers 26:11 and Exodus 6:24.

- **Numbers 26:11** Notwithstanding the children of Korah died not.

- **Exodus 6:24** And the sons of Korah; Assir, and Elkanah, and Abiasaph: these *are* the families of the Korhites.

These sons of Korah, Assir, Elkanah, and Abiasaph, apparently escaped this fate by disassociating themselves from their father's apostasy. Their descendants were prominent in the temple worship. Nine Psalms are dedicated to the sons of Korah: Psalms 42, 44, 45, 47, 48, 49, 84, 85, and 87. They were watchmen, guards, gate keepers, and singers.

- **I Chronicles 9:14** And of the Levites; Shemaiah the son of Hasshub, the son of Azrikam, the son of Hashabiah, of the sons of Merari;

- **I Chronicles 9:15** And Bakbakkar, Heresh, and Galal, and Mattaniah the son of Micah, the son of Zichri, the son of Asaph;

- **I Chronicles 9:16** And Obadiah the son of Shemaiah, the son of Galal, the son of Jeduthun, and Berechiah the son of Asa, the son of Elkanah, that dwelt in the villages of the Netophathites.

- **I Chronicles 9:17** And the porters *were,* Shallum, and Akkub, and Talmon, and Ahiman, and their brethren: Shallum *was* the chief;

- **I Chronicles 9:18** Who hitherto *waited* in the king's gate eastward: they *were* porters in the companies of the children of Levi.

- **I Chronicles 9:19** And Shallum the son of Kore, the son of Ebiasaph, the son of Korah, and his brethren, of the house of his father, the Korahites, *were* over the work of the service, keepers of the gates of the tabernacle: and their fathers, *being* over the host of the LORD, *were* keepers of the entry.

- **I Chronicles 9:20** And Phinehas the son of Eleazar was the ruler over them in time past, *and* the LORD *was* with him.

- **I Chronicles 9:21** *And* Zechariah the son of Meshelemiah *was* porter of the door of the tabernacle of the congregation.

- **I Chronicles 9:22** All these *which were* chosen to be porters in the gates *were* two hundred and twelve. These were reckoned by their genealogy in their villages, whom David and Samuel the seer did ordain in their set office.

- **I Chronicles 9:23** So they and their children *had* the oversight of the gates of the house of the LORD, *namely,* the house of the tabernacle, by wards.

- **I Chronicles 9:24** In four quarters were the porters, toward the east, west, north, and south.

- **I Chronicles 9:25** And their brethren, *which were* in their villages, *were* to come after seven days from time to time with them.

- **I Chronicles 9:26** For these Levites, the four chief porters, were in *their* set office, and were over the chambers and treasuries of the house of God.

- **I Chronicles 9:27** And they lodged round about the house of God, because the charge *was* upon them, and the opening thereof every morning *pertained* to them.

- **I Chronicles 9:28** And *certain* of them had the charge of the ministering vessels, that they should bring them in and out by tale.

- **I Chronicles 9:29** *Some* of them also *were* appointed to oversee the vessels, and all the instruments of the sanctuary, and the fine flour, and the wine, and the oil, and the frankincense, and the spices.

- **I Chronicles 9:30** And *some* of the sons of the priests made the ointment of the spices.
- **I Chronicles 9:31** And Mattithiah, *one* of the Levites, who *was* the firstborn of Shallum the Korahite, had the set office over the things that were made in the pans.
- **I Chronicles 9:32** And *other* of their brethren, of the sons of the Kohathites, *were* over the shewbread, to prepare *it* every sabbath.
- **I Chronicles 9:33** And these *are* the singers, chief of the fathers of the Levites, *who remaining* in the chambers *were* free: for they were employed in *that* work day and night.
- **I Chronicles 9:34** These chief fathers of the Levites *were* chief throughout their generations; these dwelt at Jerusalem.

What about the families of the leaders of the rebellion? They all perished from among the congregation.

- **Numbers 16:27** So they gat up from the tabernacle of Korah, Dathan, and Abiram, on every side: and Dathan and Abiram came out, and stood in the door of their tents, and their wives, and their sons, and their little children.
- **Numbers 16:28** And Moses said, Hereby ye shall know that the LORD hath sent me to do all these works; for *I have* not *done them* of mine own mind.
- **Numbers 16:29** If these men die the common death of all men, or if they be visited after the visitation of all men; *then* the LORD hath not sent me.

- **Numbers 16:30** But if the LORD make a new thing, and the earth open her mouth, and swallow them up, with all that *appertain* unto them, and they go down quick into the pit; then ye shall understand that these men have provoked the LORD.
- **Numbers 16:31** And it came to pass, as he had made an end of speaking all these words, that the ground clave asunder that *was* under them:
- **Numbers 16:32** And the earth opened her mouth, and swallowed them up, and their houses, and all the men that *appertained* unto Korah, and all *their* goods.
- **Numbers 16:33** They, and all that *appertained* to them, went down alive into the pit, and the earth closed upon them: and they perished from among the congregation.

What about the 250 princes of the assembly? Fire from the Lord consumed them.

- **Numbers 16:35** And there came out a fire from the LORD, and consumed the two hundred and fifty men that offered incense.

Korah's sin caused the death of 14,700 Israelites besides those that died about the matter of Korah.

- **Numbers 16:49** Now they that died in the plague were fourteen thousand and seven hundred, beside them that died about the matter of Korah.

Surely these things are written to warn people of today.

Chapter 11

XI.   *Degrading Conduct – vs. 12-13*

- **Jude 1:12** These are spots in your feasts of charity, when they feast with you, feeding themselves without fear: clouds *they are* without water, carried about of winds; trees whose fruit withereth, without fruit, twice dead, plucked up by the roots;
- **Jude 1:13** Raging waves of the sea, foaming out their own shame; wandering stars, to whom is reserved the blackness of darkness for ever.

Jude is not speaking of those outside the church who make no profession of knowing Jesus Christ an openly opposed to the truth of the Bible. He is speaking of ungodly, wicked, worldly, covetous leaders inside the church who make their profession of faith a cover for their sins.

In verse 12, the word "spots" refers to hidden rocks and describes a ledge or reef of rock reaching up from below the surface of the ocean. The word "spots" here means sunken rocks or "hidden reefs" which while hidden from view can run a ship aground and destroy it. These apostates in the church were like unfeeling rocks. In these love feasts, it was the practice in the early church to come together weekly to a common fellowship meal. These apostates perverted the feasts for their own ends and used to promote immorality.

Jude describes these apostates with five different

descriptions in verses 12 and 13.

1. Spots or hidden, sunken rocks
   a. Deceptive
   b. Dangerous
   c. Destructive
   d. No fear of God
   e. No reverence for God

2. Clouds without water
   a. Without grace
   b. Without truth
   c. Without blessing
   d. They are empty
   e. Useless
   f. Unstable
   g. Carried about of winds controlled by demons

3. Trees whose fruit withereth
   a. Late autumn trees
   b. Fruitless
   c. Barren profession
   d. Has only leaves
   e. Nothing for God's glory
   f. Uprooted
   g. Twice dead suggesting the second death of Revelation 20:14

4. Raging waves of the sea

a. Restlessness

- **Isaiah 57:20** But the wicked *are* like the troubled sea, when it cannot rest, whose waters cast up mire and dirt.

- **Isaiah 57:21** *There is* no peace, saith my God, to the wicked.

b. Wickedness against Christ

c. Shamefulness

d. Empty Foam

- **Philippians 3:18** (For many walk, of whom I have told you often, and now tell you even weeping, *that they are* the enemies of the cross of Christ:

- **Philippians 3:19** Whose end *is* destruction, whose God *is their* belly, and *whose* glory *is* in their shame, who mind earthly things.)

5. Wandering stars

a. Like a shooting star, meteor, comet

i. Shine for a while then pass into darkness

b. They are out of course

i. Heading into outer darkness forever with no return

These evil ones have turned from the Son of God. They are dangerous like sunken rocks, like clouds without rain, like the raging waves of the sea or ocean, and like a shooting star out of its course and they are heading into outer darkness alone forever, with no return!

Those who follow Jesus Christ will have the light of life and will shine as the stars forever.

- **John 8:12** Then spake Jesus again unto them, saying, I am the light of the world: he that followeth me shall not walk in darkness, but shall have the light of life.

- **Daniel 12:3** And they that be wise shall shine as the brightness of the firmament; and they that turn many to righteousness as the stars for ever and ever.

The lost have a hopeless end, but believers have an endless hope! Which future do you have?

Chapter 12

XII.   Retribution – vs. 14-15

- **Jude 1:14** And Enoch also, the seventh from Adam, prophesied of these, saying, Behold, the Lord cometh with ten thousands of his saints,
- **Jude 1:15** To execute judgment upon all, and to convince all that are ungodly among them of all their ungodly deeds which they have ungodly committed, and of all their hard *speeches* which ungodly sinners have spoken against him.

A. Enoch's Person

Let us notice a few things about Enoch.

1. His conversion at age 65

- **Genesis 5:21** And Enoch lived sixty and five years, and begat Methuselah:

2. He walked with God three hundred years

- **Genesis 5:22** And Enoch walked with God after he begat Methuselah three hundred years, and begat sons and daughters:

3. He pleased God

- **Hebrews 11:5** By faith Enoch was translated that he should not see death; and was not found, because God had translated him: for before his translation he had this testimony, that he pleased God.

4. He prophesied

- **Jude 1:14** And Enoch also, the seventh from Adam, prophesied of these, saying, Behold, the Lord cometh with ten thousands of his saints,

5. His name means dedicated

What a wonderful testimony! His life backed up his preaching. This is very important. It is just the opposite of those false teachers who had departed from the faith. Their lives were full of wickedness.

Enoch is the seventh from Adam. The names are given in Genesis 5. They are Adam, Seth, Enos, Cainan, Mahalaleel, Jared, and Enoch. Seven is the number of perfection, completeness, the number of the book of Revelation and the number of end times. God demonstrated in Enoch what He wanted to and will do in the church in the time of the end.

Enoch points to those who break their appointment with death and experience translation (rapture) power as told in I Corinthians and I Thessalonians.

- **I Corinthians 15:51** Behold, I shew you a

mystery; We shall not all sleep, but we shall all be changed,

- **I Thessalonians 4:13** But I would not have you to be ignorant, brethren, concerning them which are asleep, that ye sorrow not, even as others which have no hope.
- **I Thessalonians 4:14** For if we believe that Jesus died and rose again, even so them also which sleep in Jesus will God bring with him.
- **I Thessalonians 4:15** For this we say unto you by the word of the Lord, that we which are alive *and* remain unto the coming of the Lord shall not prevent them which are asleep.
- **I Thessalonians 4:16** For the Lord himself shall descend from heaven with a shout, with the voice of the archangel, and with the trump of God: and the dead in Christ shall rise first:
- **I Thessalonians 4:17** Then we which are alive *and* remain shall be caught up together with them in the clouds, to meet the Lord in the air: and so shall we ever be with the Lord.
- **I Thessalonians 4:18** Wherefore comfort one another with these words.

Enoch was caught up to heaven prior to the flood just as the church will be raptured to heaven before the great tribulation begins.

- **I Thessalonians** 1:10 And to wait for his Son from heaven, whom he raised from the dead, *even* Jesus, which delivered us from the wrath to come.

- **I Thessalonians** 5:9 For God hath not appointed us to wrath, but to obtain salvation by our Lord Jesus Christ,

B. Enoch's Prophecy

This is not given in Genesis 5, but the Spirit of God inspired Jude to record Enoch's words. Some scholars say Jude got his information from the non-canonical book of Enoch. Jude was writing by the inspiration of the Holy Spirit of God and he was prophesying by the same Holy Spirit.

It is no mystery how Enoch could know what the end time would be like and it is no mystery how Jude could know what Enoch prophesied. It is all based on inspiration from the Holy Spirit of God.

- **II Peter 1:20** Knowing this first, that no prophecy of the scripture is of any private interpretation.
- **II Peter 1:21** For the prophecy came not in old time by the will of man: but holy men of God spake *as they were* moved by the Holy Ghost.

All scripture is given by inspiration of God.

- **II Timothy 3:16** All scripture *is* given by inspiration of God, and *is* profitable for doctrine, for reproof, for correction, for instruction in righteousness:

Enoch's son name, "Methuselah", means "when he dies it

shall come" and foretold the coming judgment of the flood. Methuselah lived 969 years, longer than any human being and he died the year of the flood.

C. The Second Coming of Jesus

- **Jude 1:14** And Enoch also, the seventh from Adam, prophesied of these, saying, Behold, the Lord cometh with ten thousands of his saints,

- **Jude 1:15** To execute judgment upon all, and to convince all that are ungodly among them of all their ungodly deeds which they have ungodly committed, and of all their hard *speeches* which ungodly sinners have spoken against him.

1. Assurance of His coming
    a. "Behold the Lord cometh"

2. Attendants at His coming
    a. "with ten thousands of his saints"

3. Aim of His coming
    a. "To execute judgment"

4. Convince
    a. "to convince all"
    b. The Lord will convince or convict the ungodly of all their ungodly words and deeds spoken against him.

5. Ungodly
    a. "Ungodly" means one who has no reverence

for sacred things, godless, without fear or reverence before God.

b. Not merely the irreligious, but he who actually practices the opposite of what God demands.

6. Hard speeches

a. "Hard speeches" means harsh, hard things, opposition, injuriousness, fierce, speaking roughly.

b. God's righteous judgment shall fall upon men not only for their ungodly deeds, but for their harsh words against Him, His person, His blood, His righteousness, His ministers, and His people.

Chapter 13

XIII. Recognizing False Teachers and Preachers – vs. 16

- **Jude 1:16** These are murmurers, complainers, walking after their own lusts; and their mouth speaketh great swelling *words,* having men's persons in admiration because of advantage.

1. Their Attitude – Murmurers

Apostate teachers are characterized by their complaining against the Word of God, discontent, sullen, rebellion, and stubborn disobedience.

2. Their Accusation – Complainers

They find fault with one's lot. True believers in Jesus Christ will not complain about the station of life to which the Lord has called them. Paul said he had learned to be content.

- **Philippians 4:11** Not that I speak in respect of want: for I have learned, in whatsoever state I am, *therewith* to be content.

They are always murmuring against Jesus Christ and complaining against His followers. Beware of murmuring and complaining. It could suggest departure from the Word of God and the beginning of apostasy.

3. Their Activity – Walking

The apostates do as their father, the devil, who walks about seeking to devour.

- **I Peter 5:8** … walketh about, seeking whom he may devour:

The apostates are walking after their own lusts. They thrive on sinful lustful things. An apostate does not have spiritual life. He scornfully rejects the Holy Spirit and has committed one of the Bible's unpardonable sins, therefore, he can never be saved. All he has left is lust so he walks after it. His whole life is controlled by lust.

4. Their Arrogance

"Their mouth speaketh great swelling *words*". Swelling means extravagant, overbearing, pride, or self-importance. Error is at home in this world, therefore, has advantage over truth.

Someone has said a lie will travel around the world while truth is getting its boots on. Truth is like cotton, corn, peas, and beans; you have to cultivate it. While error is like weeds and undesirable grass, it will grow if left alone.

Let us notice the Apostle Peter's comments on this principle in II Peter chapter 2.

a. They have forsaken the right way and gone astray.

- **II Peter 2:15** Which have forsaken the right way, and are gone astray, following the way of Balaam *the son* of Bosor, who loved the wages of unrighteousness;

b. They speak great swelling words of vanity.

- **II Peter 2:18** For when they speak great swelling *words* of vanity, they allure through the lusts of the flesh, *through much* wantonness, those that were clean escaped from them who live in error.

c. They promise liberty when they themselves are in corrupt bondage.

- **II Peter 2:19** While they promise them liberty, they themselves are the servants of corruption: for of whom a man is overcome, of the same is he brought in bondage.

d. They have some knowledge of the right way, turned from it, and became entangled again and were overcome.

- **II Peter 2:20** For if after they have escaped the pollutions of the world through the knowledge of the Lord and Saviour Jesus Christ, they are again entangled therein, and overcome, the latter end is worse with them than the beginning.

- **II Peter 2:21** For it had been better for them not to have known the way of righteousness, than, after they have known *it,* to turn from the holy commandment delivered unto them.

e. They are like sick dogs and like sows wallowing in mud.

- **II Peter 2:22** But it is happened unto them according to the true proverb, The dog *is* turned to his own vomit again; and the sow that was washed to her wallowing in the mire.

They are unclean and vile in the sight of a Holy God having men's persons in admiration because of advantage. They flatter men for what they can get from them. They are masters in the art of flattery, thereby, gaining a following for themselves and a comfortable income, admiring, showing respect of persons, introducing and presenting people on the platform of "build up" as the world does. Personality preachers are perhaps a sign of apostasy. This is how false teachers and false prophets operate.

Chapter 14

XIV. Recognition – vs. 17-19

- **Jude 1:17** But, beloved, remember ye the words which were spoken before of the apostles of our Lord Jesus Christ;
- **Jude 1:18** How that they told you there should be mockers in the last time, who should walk after their own ungodly lusts.
- **Jude 1:19** These be they who separate themselves, sensual, having not the Spirit.

The apostles of our Lord had clearly warned about the last days. Ungodly mockers would despise God and true believers.

1. The Warning

- **Jude 1:17** But, beloved, remember ye the words which were spoken before of the apostles of our Lord Jesus Christ;

Let us remember the words of the Bible. They are the words that God would have us to know.

a. Paul warned the Ephesian elders. Some apostates were already in the Church.
  - **Acts 20:29** For I know this, that after my departing shall grievous wolves enter in among you, not sparing the flock.

- **Acts 20:30** Also of your own selves shall men arise, speaking perverse things, to draw away disciples after them.
- **Acts 20:31** Therefore watch, and remember, that by the space of three years I ceased not to warn every one night and day with tears.

b. Paul warned Timothy. Some will depart from the faith.

- **I Timothy 4:1** Now the Spirit speaketh expressly, that in the latter times some shall depart from the faith, giving heed to seducing spirits, and doctrines of devils;
- **I Timothy 4:2** Speaking lies in hypocrisy; having their conscience seared with a hot iron;

c. Paul wrote with certainty of the godlessness in the last days.

- **II Timothy 3:1** This know also, that in the last days perilous times shall come.

The word "know" means to know, beware, perceive, learn, understand, to get a knowledge of. The word "perilous" means hard to bear, grievous, painful, fierce, not tame. These are said of the characteristics of the last days.

Let us look, watch, work, and wait until Jesus comes to take us to our eternal home in heaven.

- **Titus 2:13** Looking for that blessed hope, and the glorious appearing of the great God and our Saviour Jesus Christ;

- **Mark 13:35** Watch ye therefore: for ye know not when the master of the house cometh, at even, or at midnight, or at the cockcrowing, or in the morning:
- **Mark 13:36** Lest coming suddenly he find you sleeping.
- **Mark 13:37** And what I say unto you I say unto all, Watch.

- **Matthew 5:16** Let your light so shine before men, that they may see your good works, and glorify your Father which is in heaven.

- **1Thessilonians 1:10** And to wait for his Son from heaven, whom he raised from the dead, *even* Jesus, which delivered us from the wrath to come.

2. The Walk of the apostates

- **Jude 1:18** How that they told you there should be mockers in the last time, who should walk after their own ungodly lusts.

a. They are mockers and scoffers
    - **II Peter 3:3** Knowing this first, that there shall come in the last days scoffers, walking after their own lusts,

One such teaching in particular that is disliked by the scoffer is the promise that Jesus Christ will one day return to earth the second time.

- **II Peter 3:4** And saying, Where is the promise of his coming? for since the fathers fell asleep, all things continue as *they were* from the beginning of the creation.
- **II Peter 3:5** For this they willingly are ignorant of, that by the word of God the heavens were of old, and the earth standing out of the water and in the water:

They are willingly ignorant of the Word of God.

3. Wells without water

- **Jude 1:19** These be they who separate themselves, sensual, having not the Spirit.

"These be they who separate themselves" are those who are agitators. They cause divisions in the Church. Paul told the Roman believers to mark them that cause division.

- **Romans 16:17** Now I beseech you, brethren, mark them which cause divisions and offences contrary to the doctrine which ye have learned; and avoid them.
- **Romans 16:18** For they that are such serve not our Lord Jesus Christ, but their own belly; and by good words and fair speeches deceive the hearts of the simple.

Diotrephes caused division in his day by refusing to receive the Apostle John.

- **III John 1:9** I wrote unto the church: but

Diotrephes, who loveth to have the preeminence among them, receiveth us not.

He would not receive the brethren, forbade any to receive the brethren, and would cast them out of the Church if they did receive the brethren. Diotrephes loved to have preeminence among them. Jesus Christ is the only person who is to have the preeminence in any New Testament Church.

"Sensual, having not the Spirit". Jesus speaking to the woman at Jacob's well.

- **John 4:13** Jesus answered and said unto her, Whosoever drinketh of this water shall thirst again:
- **John 4:14** But whosoever drinketh of the water that I shall give him shall never thirst; but the water that I shall give him shall be in him a well of water springing up into everlasting life.

A great many Churches just have swimming pools (i.e. entertainment) and no well of spiritual water springing up into everlasting life. All have "a spirit", but not "the Spirit". This distinguishes an apostate; he does not have the Holy Spirit.

Chapter 15

XV. *Exhortation – vs. 20-23*

- **Jude 1:20** But ye, beloved, building up yourselves on your most holy faith, praying in the Holy Ghost,
- **Jude 1:21** Keep yourselves in the love of God, looking for the mercy of our Lord Jesus Christ unto eternal life.
- **Jude 1:22** And of some have compassion, making a difference:
- **Jude 1:23** And others save with fear, pulling *them* out of the fire; hating even the garment spotted by the flesh.

- **Jude 1:3** Beloved, when I gave all diligence to write unto you of the common salvation, it was needful for me to write unto you, and exhort *you* that ye should earnestly contend for the faith which was once delivered unto the saints.

A. Our Activity – Building – vs. 20

1. **Jude 1:3** ...earnestly contend for the faith which was once delivered unto the saints.

This is illustrated in the sword of Nehemiah. Everyone with one of his hands working and the other hand held a weapon.

- **Nehemiah 4:17** They which builded on the wall,

and they that bare burdens, with those that laded, *every one* with one of his hands wrought in the work, and with the other *hand* held a weapon.

- **Nehemiah 4:18** For the builders, every one had his sword girded by his side, and *so* builded. And he that sounded the trumpet *was* by me.

2. **Jude 1:20** …building up yourselves on your most holy faith.

Neither of these two admonitions of Jude can take precedence over the other without loss. If we contend without building, or if we build without contending, we are without balance. We are giving heed to only part of the Word of God.

So how do we build ourselves up in the faith?

a. By applying the teaching of the scriptures to our lives. Paul encouraged the Ephesians elders.

- **Acts 20:32** And now, brethren, I commend you to God, and to the word of his grace, which is able to build you up, and to give you an inheritance among all them which are sanctified.

b. Your faith is increased by the Word of God.

- **Romans 10:17** So then faith *cometh* by hearing, and hearing by the word of God.

c. Obedience to the Word of God brings untold blessings.

- **James 1:25** But whoso looketh into the perfect law of liberty, and continueth *therein,* he being not a forgetful hearer, but a doer of the work, this man shall be blessed in his deed.

B. Our Attitude – Prayer – vs. 20

1. **Jude 1:20** … praying in the Holy Ghost.

Prayer in the Spirit is the prayer of believing men with their hearts open to the divine message and divine will of God.

C. Our Attention – Keeping – vs. 21

1. **Jude 1:21** Keep yourselves in the love of God…

Keeping yourselves is to attend carefully, take care of that is governed and controlled by God's love.

D. Our Anticipation – Looking – vs. 21

1. **Jude 1:21** … looking for the mercy of our Lord Jesus Christ unto eternal life.

Looking for is to receive to oneself, admit, to expect, wait for. This refers to the rapture of the Church.

- **I Thessalonians 4:13** But I would not have you to be ignorant, brethren, concerning them which are asleep, that ye sorrow not, even as others which have no hope.

- **I Thessalonians 4:14** For if we believe that Jesus died and rose again, even so them also which sleep in Jesus will God bring with him.
- **I Thessalonians 4:15** For this we say unto you by the word of the Lord, that we which are alive *and* remain unto the coming of the Lord shall not prevent them which are asleep.
- **I Thessalonians 4:16** For the Lord himself shall descend from heaven with a shout, with the voice of the archangel, and with the trump of God: and the dead in Christ shall rise first:
- **I Thessalonians 4:17** Then we which are alive *and* remain shall be caught up together with them in the clouds, to meet the Lord in the air: and so shall we ever be with the Lord.
- **I Thessalonians 4:18** Wherefore comfort one another with these words.

E. Our Affection – Compassion – vs. 22

1. **Jude 1:22** And of some have compassion …

This refers to souls that must be kept from these false teachers and their doctrines. Some need compassion, tact, delicate handling.

D. Our Action – Pulling Out – vs. 23

1. **Jude 1:23** … pulling *them* out of the fire …
This refers to souls that need other drastic measures.
   a. Those who we pluck from the fire, God has a

personal interest in.

b. We should see them as God sees them, dressed in filthy rags

- **Isaiah 64:6** But we are all as an unclean *thing,* and all our righteousnesses *are* as filthy rags; and we all do fade as a leaf; and our iniquities, like the wind, have taken us away.

Snatch these from the fire now and from the wrath to come. True faith will assure they will be safe from the fire then.

Chapter 16

XVI. Adoration – vs. 24-25

- **Jude 1:24** Now unto him that is able to keep you from falling, and to present *you* faultless before the presence of his glory with exceeding joy,
- **Jude 1:25** To the only wise God our Saviour, *be* glory and majesty, dominion and power, both now and ever. Amen.

A. Power – Able – vs. 24

1. **Jude 1:24** Now unto him that is able to keep you from falling…

God is able to keep or guard us from falling or stumbling. Now notice back in verse 1 who it is that He guards or keeps from falling.

a. To those whom Jude is writing, those sanctified by God the Father
b. The preserved ones in Jesus Christ
c. The called ones, children of God

B. Preservation – Keep – vs. 24

1. **Jude 1:24** Now unto him that is able to keep…

Keep is to watch, not to sleep, keep watch to guard. Believers are kept by the power of God

- **I Peter 1:5** Who are kept by the power of God through faith unto salvation ready to be revealed in the last time.

C. Presentation – Present you – vs. 24

1. **Jude 1:24** Now unto him that is able to keep you from falling, and to present *you*...

Now comes the sudden transition. He is able to set you before the presence of His glory. New he describes in one breath taking utterance, that moment of rapturous fulfillment of the Blessed Hope of the ages when we shall see our Lord in His glory.

D. Perfection – Faultless – vs. 24

1. **Jude 1:24** Now unto him that is able to keep you from falling, and to present *you* faultless...

Faultlessness is to present you faultless, without a blemish. Our Savior Jesus Christ is without blemish, so must we be, and shall be, when Jesus comes for us. When He resurrects the dead bodies of the saints, they will be faultless without blemish.

E. Prospect – His Presence – vs. 24

1. **Jude 1:24** Now unto him that is able to keep you from falling, and to present *you* faultless before the presence of his glory...

Jesus said that where He is, we will be also.

- **John 14:3** And if I go and prepare a place for you, I will come again, and receive you unto myself; that where I am, *there* ye may be also.

F. Pleasure – Joy – vs. 24

1. **Jude 1:24** Now unto him that is able to keep you from falling, and to present *you* faultless before the presence of his glory with exceeding joy,

- **Psalm 16:11** Thou wilt shew me the path of life: in thy presence *is* fulness of joy; at thy right hand *there are* pleasures for evermore.

In Psalm 16:11, there are four things observable:

a. A Guide – Thou
b. A Traveler – Me
c. A Way – the Path
d. The End – Life

This verse is a proper subject for a mediation. The Guide is but one, the traveler is one, they way is one, the life is the only one.

The passing sorrows of time will give place to the exceeding joys of eternity.

G. Praise – vs. 25

1. The Benediction

- **Jude 1:25** To the only wise God our Saviour, *be* glory and majesty, dominion and power, both now and ever. Amen.

Human language cannot contain the fullness of the meaning of the four words used by Jude to ascribe praise and worship to God.

a. Glory
- **Jude 1:25** To the only wise God our Saviour, *be* glory...

Glory is the brightness, the manifested excellence of God. It is a divine radiance which shines, which blinds, which cannot be endured by the unglorified human race.

- **Luke 2:9** And, lo, the angel of the Lord came upon them, and the glory of the Lord shone round about them: and they were sore afraid.
- **Acts 22:11** And when I could not see for the glory of that light, being led by the hand of them that were with me, I came into Damascus.

b. Majesty
- **Jude 1:25** To the only wise God our Saviour, *be* glory and majesty...

Majesty, a word which refers to the incomparable presence of the ruler of the universe. It suggests the omniscience (all knowing) of God.

   c. Dominion
- Jude 1:25 To the only wise God our Saviour, *be* glory and majesty, dominion...

Dominion may be said to contemplate (consider) the infinite extent of the strong rule of God throughout His universe. Dominion suggest the omnipresence (present in all places at the same time) of God.

- **Hebrews 1:3** Who being the brightness of *his* glory, and the express image of his person, and upholding all things by the word of his power...

   d. Power
- **Jude 1:25** To the only wise God our Saviour, *be* glory and majesty, dominion and power, both now and ever. Amen.

Power is the irresistible divine authority and might exercised by our God. It suggest His omnipotence; all powerful, unlimited power.

How long has God possessed these attributes? Both now and ever, before all time, and now, and forever.

We can do no better in summing up these mighty and glorious words of Jude than to say with David of old:

I Chronicles 29:11 *Thine, O LORD, is the greatness, and the power, and the glory, and the victory, and the majesty: for all that is in the heaven and in the earth is thine; thine is the kingdom, O LORD, and thou art exalted as head above all.*

BIOGRAPHY

An Exegetical Commentary on Genesis – by Thomas M. Strouse
Cushing-Malloy, Inc.

The Genesis Record – by Henry M. Morris
Baker Book House

Exploring the Epistle Jude – by John Phillips Kregel
John Phillips Kregel Publications

The Acts of the Apostates – by S. Maxwell Coder
Moody Press Publications

The Whole Realm of Rebellion, Studies in The Book of Jude – by
N. W. Hutchings
Bible Belt Publishing

Lectures on the Epistle of Jude – by William Kelly
Believers Bookshelf, Inc.

Brown-Driver-Briggs-Gesenius Hebrew and English Lexicon
Associated Publishers and Authors Inc.

The Englishman's Hebrew Concordance of The Old Testament –
by George V. Wigram
Hendrickson Publishers Inc.

Gesenius' Hebrew Chaldee Lexicon to The Old Testament
Baker Book House

Bible Doctrines – Beliefs That Matter – by Mark G. Cameron
(The Imprisoned Angels – pages 241, 242, 243)
Zondervan Publication

Practical Christian Theology – by Floyd H. Barackman
(Several Facts About Angels – page 232)
Kregal Publications

Lightning Source UK Ltd.
Milton Keynes UK
UKHW021842090223
416682UK00012B/664